James Wants to See
Everything!

by Joseph Settecasi

Illustrated by Lisa Bohart

Copyright 2021 Joseph Settecasi
All rights reserved.

No part of this publication may be reproduced,
stored in a retrieval system, transmitted in any form
or by any means, electronic, mechanical, photocopying,
recording, or otherwise, without prior written
permission of the publisher and author/illustrator.

Printed in the U.S.A. by Ingram, Nashville, TN

James Wants to See EVERYTHING!
Authored by Joseph Settecasi
Edited by Jane Brandi Johnson
Graphic design and illustrations by Lisa Bohart
Pre-press production by MJ Clark

ISBN-13: 978-0-578-81572-5
LCCN: 2020924053

Printed in January 2021

To contact Joseph Settecasi
visit his website at: josephsettecasi.com

This book is dedicated to my granddaughter James, whose love and energy for living is the inspiration for this story and to all the scientists, both past and present, for making our lives better.

<u>Hidden Words</u>

Within each two-page spread is a 'hidden word' for children to find.

These words are science concepts which relate directly to the story. More importantly, they provide scientific information that can be further studied and explored with a parent or teacher.

A key to the hidden words can be found at the back of the book.

James Wants to See EVERYTHING! is about us and how we see the world around us.

Joseph Settecasi

Everyone knew it. Everyone knew that James was the most curious girl they had ever met.
She wanted to see EVERYTHING.
Yes! James, the spirited girl with a passion for life, wants to see everything in person—**with her own eyes**—not just on a television screen or pictures in a book.

One night, just minutes before sleep, James wrote a list of some of the things she wanted to see. She tucked it under her pillow with a plan to show it to her dad at breakfast.

He would know just what she needed to do.

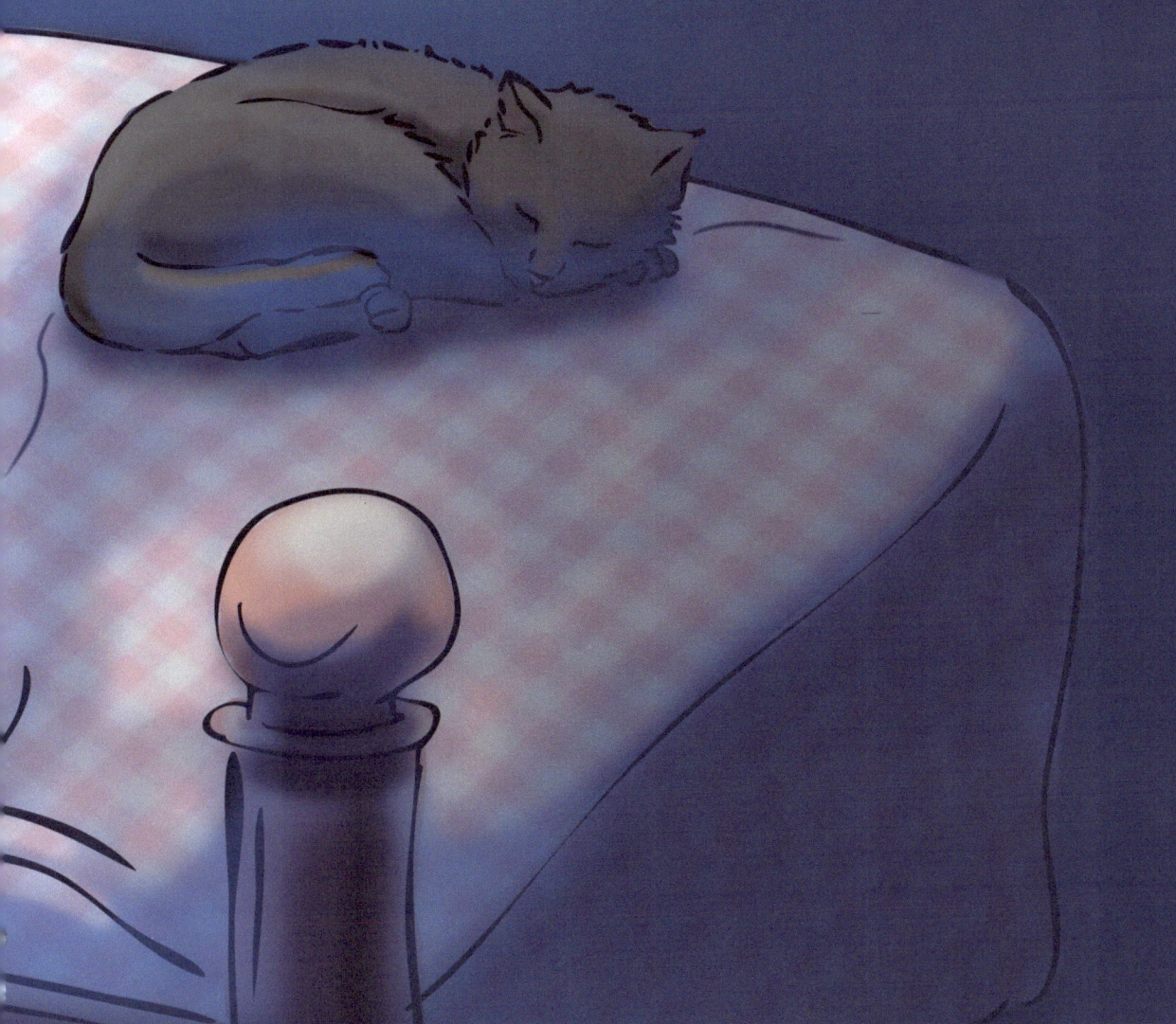

"Good morning Dad," says James. "Good morning James."

"What's that piece of paper in your hand?" asks Dad.

"I made a list of some amazing things I want to see," says James.

"Can I take a peek?" asks Dad.

On the list were the Pacific Ocean, an elephant in Africa, a glacier in Alaska, and the Statue of Liberty.

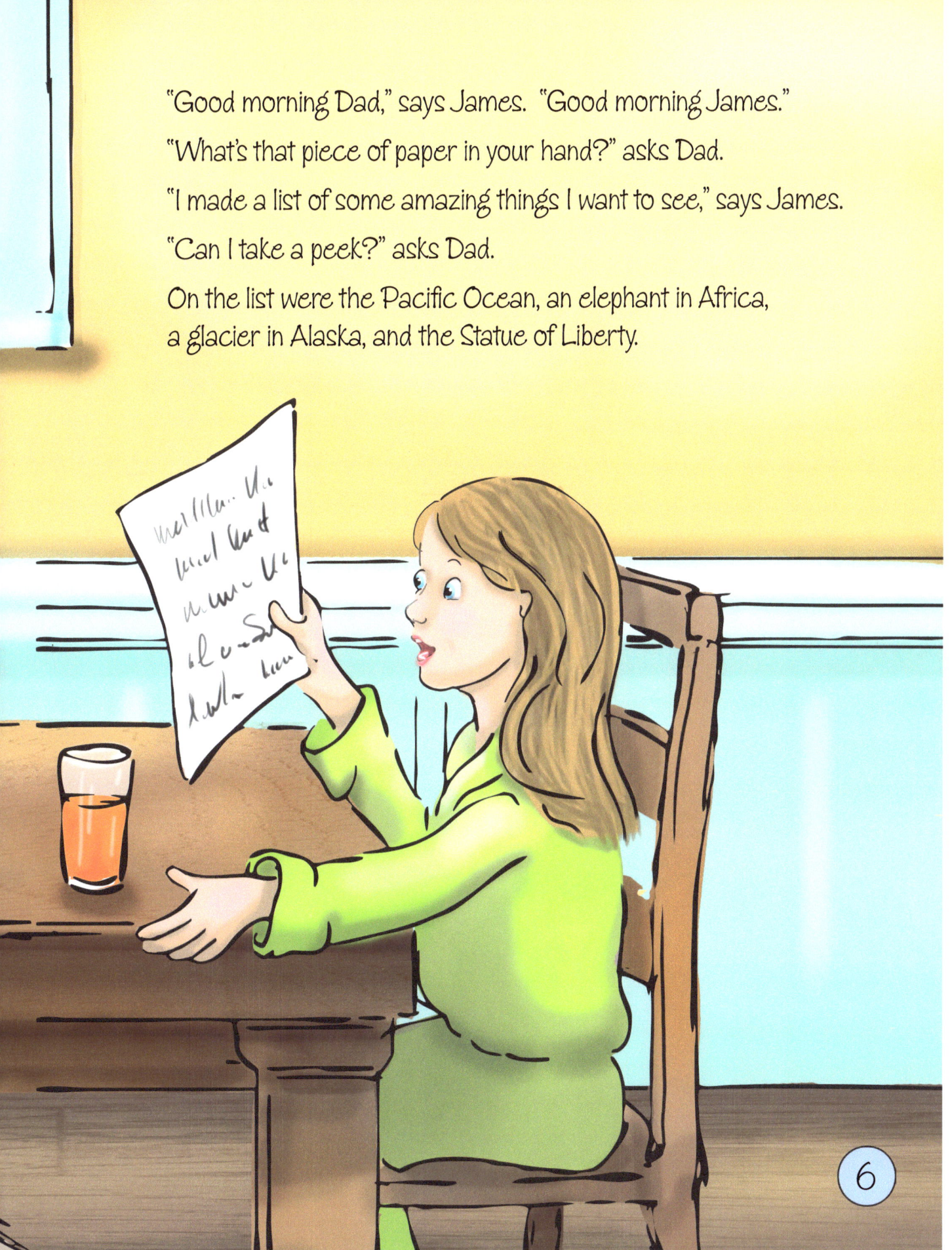

"I can take you to all these wonderful places James, and you can see them for yourself," says Dad.

"But, did you know there are also many things that our eyes can't see? **They are invisible to us.** We know they are real, but we can't see them," says Dad.

"WHAT?" says James. "I want to see EVERYTHING!"

That night at bedtime, James was still thinking about what her dad had said.

The thought kept echoing in her head.

There are many things that our eyes can't see.
There are many things that our eyes can't see.
There are many things that our eyes can't see.......

Soon James was fast asleep.

That night, James has a dream that her cat sneaks into her room.

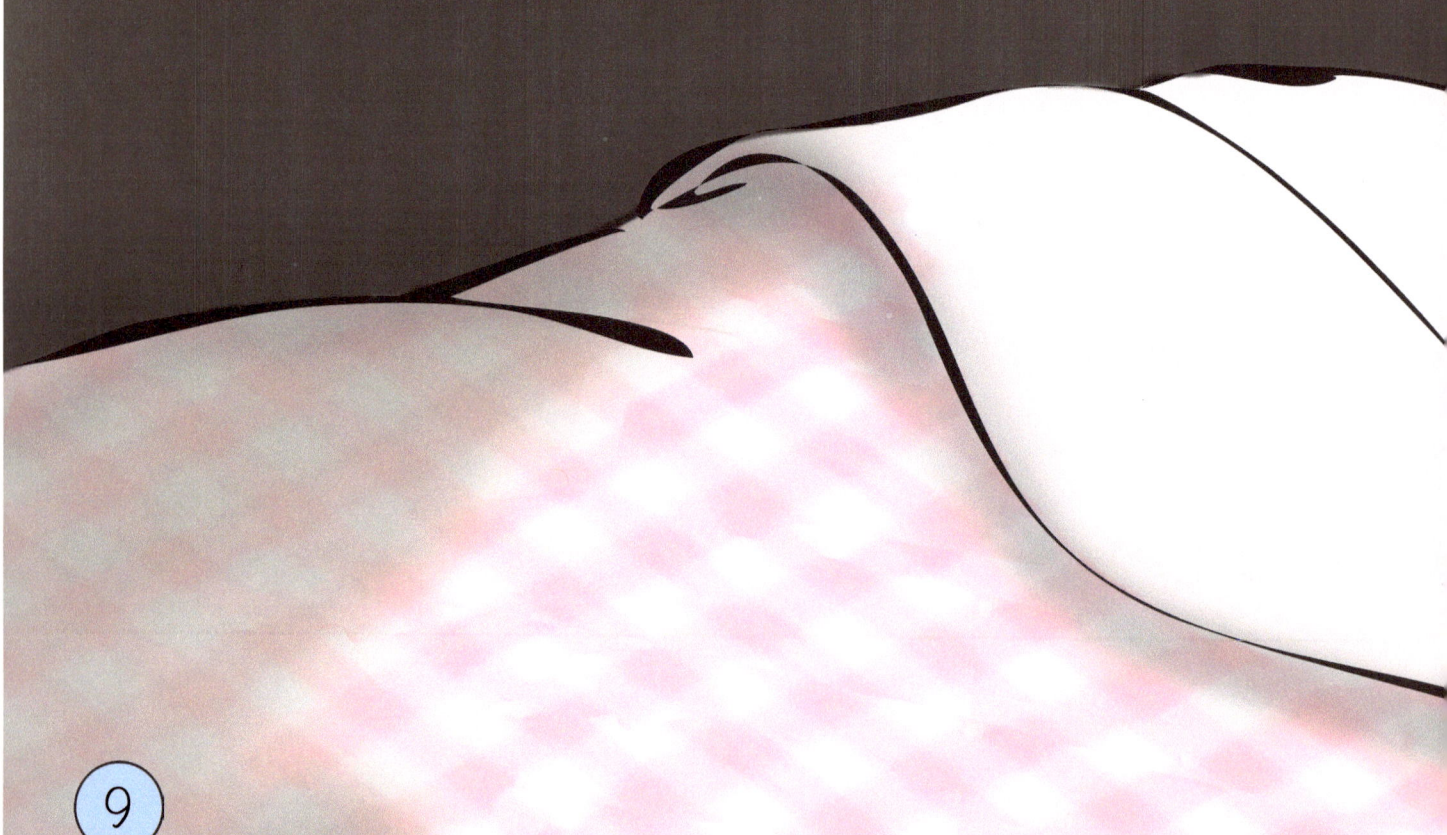

"Why are you sad?" asks Max.

"My dad said that many things are invisible but……. I want to see EVERYTHING," says James.

"Don't worry James. I have just what you need," says Max. James watches closely as Max reaches behind his back and snatches something out.

"What are those?" asks James. "These are **MAGIC GLASSES.**

Whoever puts them on can see all kinds of things that are invisible," says Max.

"That's fantastic Max! I want to try them. What should I do?" asks James.

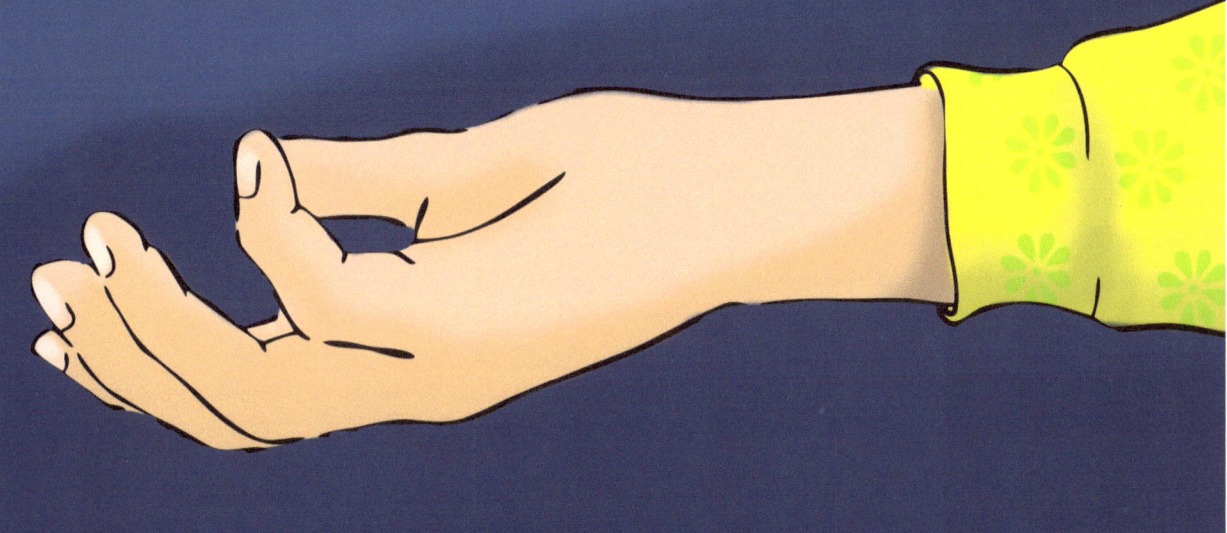

"Close your eyes, and think of a place that you want to see," says Max.

"Now hold my hand, and I'll take you there."

When James opens her eyes, she is standing up, looking out at the Pacific Ocean.

"What do you see?" asks Max.

"I see beautiful blue water and big waves," says James.

"Put on the magic glasses," says Max. "**Now** what do you see?"

"OH WOW," says James. "I see millions of tiny livings things in the water!"

"That's Plankton," says Max. "Plankton is the cool name for all the plants and animals that live in the ocean but are too small to see."

"Plankton is the stuff that many sea animals, like fish and whales, eat. Without Plankton, there would be no life in the Ocean," says Max.

"Nice to see you, Plankton. Thank you for making our Oceans so full of life," says James.

"That was great Max. Let's go somewhere else," says James.

"Close your eyes, and think of a place that you want to see," says Max.

"Now hold my hand, and I'll take you there."

When James opens her eyes, she is standing on the bank of a river.

"What do you see?" asks Max.

"I see a family of beautiful elephants washing themselves in the river."

"Put on the magic glasses," says Max. "**Now** what do you see?"

"**YUK!** I see tiny little things on the skin of one of the elephants."

"You are seeing Germs. They are not hurting the elephant," says Max.

"Some Germs are helpful to us, but some germs can cause things like colds or sore throats," says Max.

"That's why we wash our hands before eating. That's why we all take baths. Washing with soap helps to keep the **bad** Germs away," says Max.

"Nice to see you, good Germs. Thanks for helping to keep me healthy," says James.

"That was great. Let's go somewhere else," says James.

"Close your eyes, and think of a place you want to see," says Max.

"Now hold my hand, and I'll take you there."

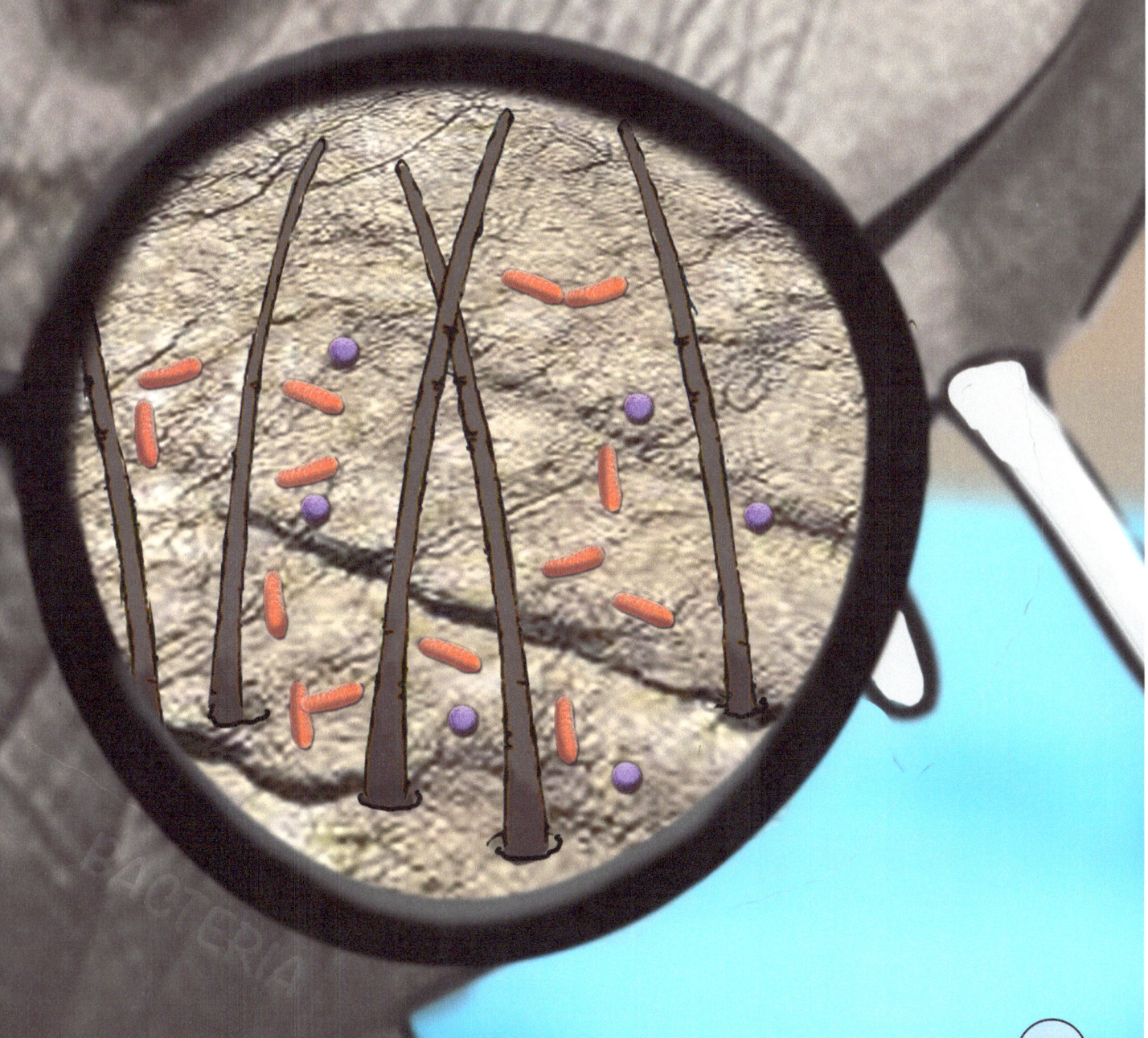

When James opens her eyes, she is standing on the top of a glacier in Alaska.

"What do you see?" asks Max.

"I see a GIGANTIC block of ice and a Mama Polar Bear with her Cub," says James.

"Put on the magic glasses," says Max. "**Now** what do you see?"

"Well, I don't see anything different, but I feel like I'm **Moving**," says James.

"Exactly!" says Max. "All glaciers Move, but their movement is too slow to see with your eyes."

"During the last Ice Age, moving glaciers created many of the land features on Planet Earth. The Great Lakes and the Mississippi River are two good examples," says Max.

"Nice to feel you move, Glacier. Thank you for making such beautiful landscapes on Planet Earth," says James.

"That was great. Let's go somewhere else," says James.

"Close your eyes, and think of a place you want to see," says Max. "Now hold my hand, and I'll take you there."

When James opens her eyes, she is standing inside the crown of the Statue of Liberty in New York City.

"What do you see?" asks Max. "I see a beautiful city and a Statue that welcomes all people to America," says James.

"James, take hold of this red ball. What do you think will happen when you let go of it from way up here?" asks Max.

"Oh Max, that's easy! The ball will fall straight down to the ground," says James.

"Put on the magic glasses," says Max. "**Now** what do you see?"

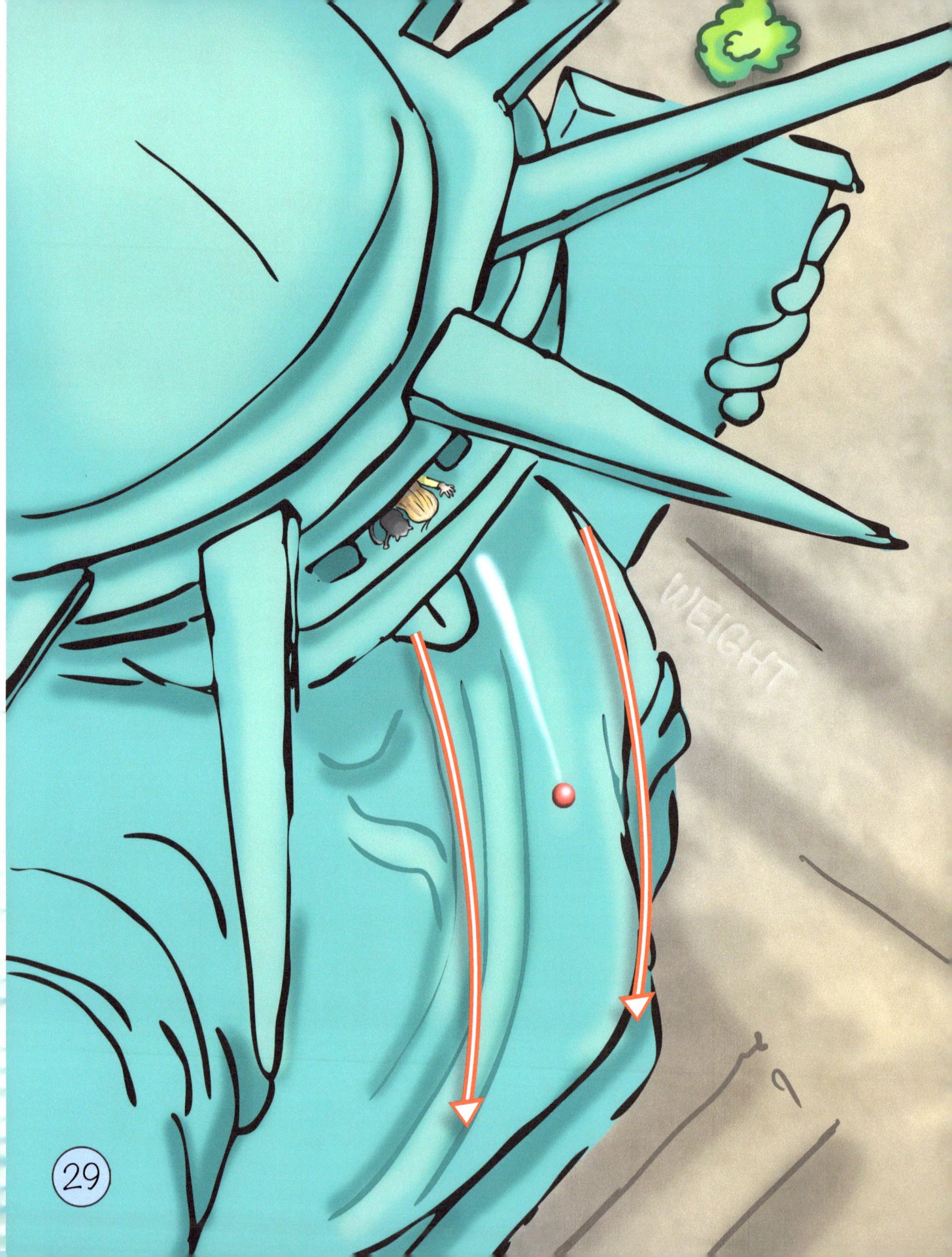

"I see powerful lines moving toward the Earth."

"What are those lines?" asks James.

"Gravity," says Max.

"Gravity is the invisible force that pulls everything including you, me, and the ball to center of the Earth. Gravity holds everything on Earth in its place," says Max.

"Gravity actually keeps the air we breathe from floating away. Without gravity there would be no Life on Planet Earth," says Max.

"Nice to see you, Gravity. Thank you for keeping Max and me from floating away," says James.

"What's next?" asks James.

"It's almost morning James. It's time for us to head home," says Max.

The next morning, Dad comes into James' room to wake her up for school.

"James, I think you had a dream last night. I heard you talking in your sleep," says Dad.

"What was the dream about?" asks Dad.

"I had a dream that Max gave me a magic pair of glasses so that I could see invisible things," says James.

"That sounds fun. So, why does this make you look sad?" asks Dad.

"Because it was only a dream, I will **never ever, ever, ever** see things that are invisible again. **MAGIC GLASSES ARE NOT REAL!**" says James.

"Oh, that's NOT quite true," says Dad.

"What do you mean, Dad?" asks James.

"Many things are invisible to us James, but scientists have invented instruments and machines that are just like MAGIC GLASSES. These special inventions bring magic to our eyes! We can see things with them in very special ways."

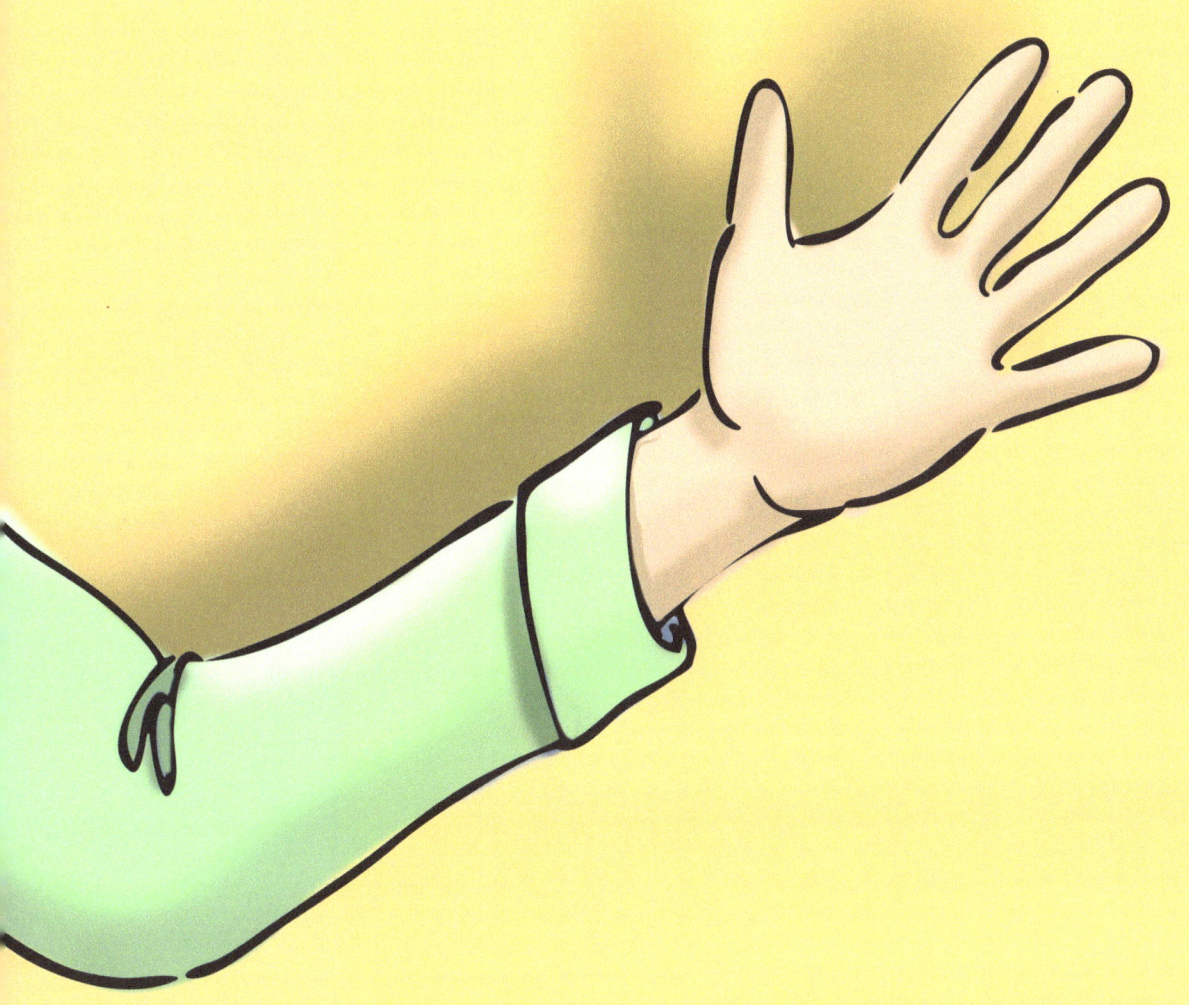

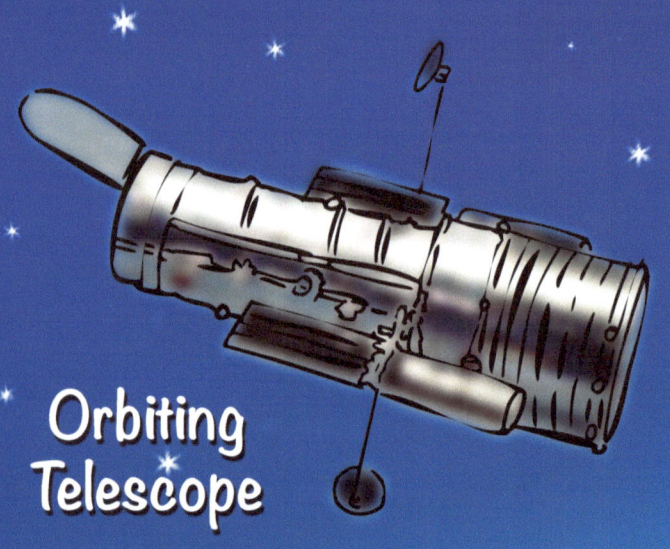

Orbiting Telescope

SpaceX Rocket

"With a microscope, you can see very small living things like Plankton and Germs."

"With a telescope, you can see far-away stars, moons, and planets."

MRI

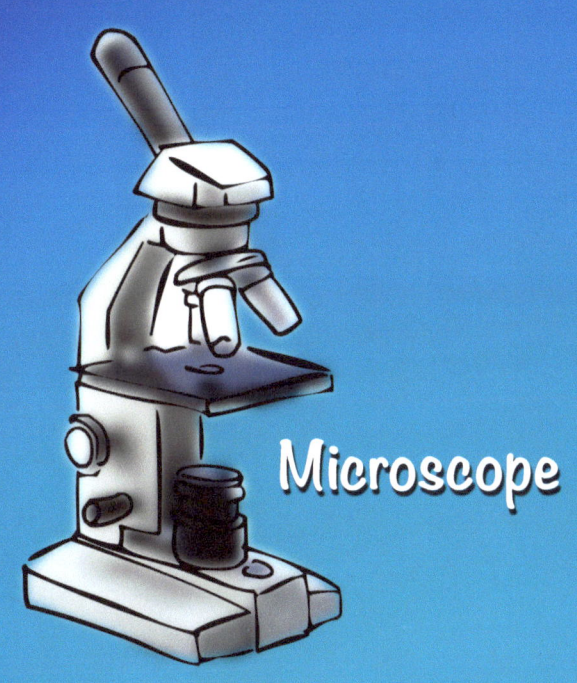
Microscope

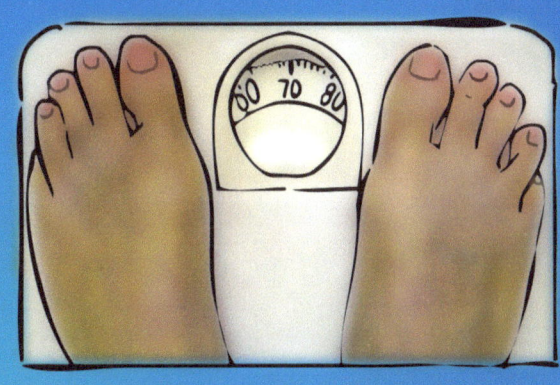
Gravity

"Special scientific instruments allow us to see the movement of glaciers, and measure the force of Gravity."

"X-ray and MRI machines can peek inside the human body," says Dad.

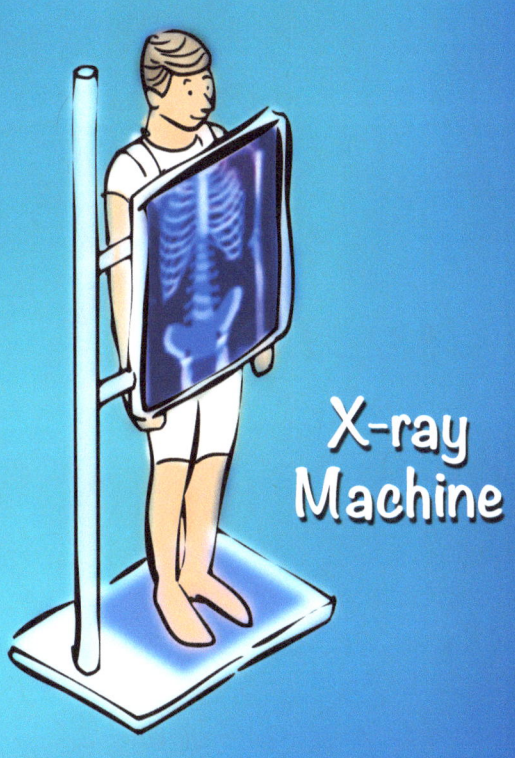
X-ray Machine

Telescope

"Magic glasses are real!" says James.

"YES, THEY ARE!" says Dad with a big smile.

"And thanks to scientists who invent new technology, we are seeing more and more invisible things every day."

"Thanks Dad! You're GREAT!" says James.

"James, I'm really glad that **YOU** are not invisible," says dad with playful look on his face.

"Why?" asks James.

"Then how would I keep an **EYE** on you?"

"Dad, you are just too funny!"

Key to Hidden Words

page 1	**BIOLUMINESCENCE**	Bio means life; luminescence means producing light without heat. Fireflies use bioluminescence to find each other for mating.
page 3	**LIGHT**	In order for humans to see an object, visible light rays from the sun or a lamp, must reflect off the object into the eye. The reflected light enters the eye and is focused to strike the light-sensitive area of the eye called the **retina**. The retina receives the light and changes the light into nerve signals that are sent to the brain.
page 5	**EARTH**	The Earth is the third planet from the Sun and the only astronomical object known to have life. About 29% of Earth's surface is land (continents and islands). The remaining 71% is covered with water (oceans, lakes, and rivers).
page 8	**MICROSCOPIC**	The scientific word that means too small to be seen with the human eye.
page 10	**REM**	REM means **R**apid **E**ye **M**ovement. REM sleep happens about 90 minutes after you have fallen asleep. The brain is very active at this point and that is when dreams happen.
page 11	**FELINE**	A Feline is any member of the cat family. If your cat kneads on you or touches your face with its paws while snuggling up to you, it is putting its scent on you to show how much it loves you.
page 13	**IMAGINATION**	Without this creative **power** we may never have had the internet, smartphones, airplanes, and other amazing technology we rely on every day. Simply put, imagination is the key ingredient to the advancement of our world.
page 16	**MAGELLAN**	Explorer, Ferdinand Magellan named the Pacific Ocean in the 16th century. He called this body of water pacific, due to the calmness of the water at the time (Pacific means peaceful). The Pacific Ocean has the deepest point on Earth. It is called the Challenger Deep and is 36,000 feet down.
page 18	**PHYTOPLANKTON**	Phytoplankton means plant plankton and Zooplankton means animal plankton. Phytoplankton in our oceans produce more than **half of the Oxygen** that we breathe on Earth.
page 20	**TRUNK**	An elephant's trunk is actually a long nose used for smelling, breathing, trumpeting, drinking, and grabbing things. The trunk alone contains about 40,000 muscles.

page 22	**BACTERIA**	Bacteria is the scientific name for germs. Our bodies have trillions of "good" bacteria that live mostly in our digestive system. Not only do we live in harmony with these bacteria, but they are absolutely necessary for our survival.
page 24	**32 DEGREES**	The temperature that water freezes on the Fahrenheit scale.
page 26	**CLIMATE CHANGE**	Humans are increasingly influencing the **climate and the Earth's temperature** by burning fossil fuels, cutting down rainforests, and farming livestock. This adds enormous amounts of greenhouse gases to those naturally occurring in the atmosphere, increasing the greenhouse effect and **global warming**. The Earth's warming is causing rising sea levels and the melting of glaciers in Alaska, Greenland, and Antarctica.
page 27	**FRANCE**	The Statue of Liberty was a gift of friendship from the people of France to the United States and is recognized as a symbol of freedom and democracy. The Statue of Liberty was dedicated on October 28, 1886.
page 29	**WEIGHT**	Weight is determined by your mass (the matter in you) **and by the strength of gravity**. If you weigh 120 pounds on Earth, you would weigh only 20 pounds on the moon. Even though your mass would be the same, the moon is much smaller than the Earth, so the gravitational pull on you would be much less.
page 31	**JOURNAL**	If you want to remember a dream, it is best to keep a dream journal. A dream journal is a notebook where you write down your dreams as soon as you wake up.
page 33	**GALILEO**	Galileo Galilei was an Italian astronomer, physicist, and engineer. Galileo has been called the "father of observational astronomy," the "father of modern physics," and the "father of modern science." His most famous invention was the telescope.
page 35	**HUBBLE**	**Edwin Hubble**, for whom the Hubble Space Telescope is named, was one of the leading astronomers of the twentieth century. His discovery, in the 1920s, that billions of galaxies exist beyond our own Milky Way galaxy revolutionized our understanding of the universe and our place within it.
page 37	**BRAD**	Brad is James's dad.

"Vision is the art of seeing what is invisible to others."
Jonathan Swift

www.ingramcontent.com/pod-product-compliance
Lightning Source LLC
Chambersburg PA
CBHW041154290426

44108CB00002B/60